AF407941

Budget
PLANNER

Cut expenses, not dreams

This planner belongs to:

K Creations

more to explore:

amazon.com/author/kcreations

SAVINGS TRACKER

YEAR OF	SAVING FOR	AMOUNT NEEDED

MONTH	WEEK 1	WEEK 2	WEEK 3	WEEK 4	TOTAL
JANUARY					
FEBRUARY					
MARCH					
APRIL					
MAY					
JUNE					
JULY					
AUGUST					
SEPTEMBER					
OCTOBER					
NOVEMBER					
DECEMBER					

MONTHLY BUDGET

JAN FEB MAR APR MAY JUN JUL AUG SEP OCT NOV DEC

INCOME

BILLS/UTILITIES		

INSURANCE

SHOPPING
WK 1
WK 2
WK 3
WK 4

GROCERIES/EATING OUT		

DEBT

TRANSPORTATION
WK 1
WK 2
WK 3
WK 4

SAVINGS

DONATIONS

OTHER EXPENSES			

TOTAL INCOME:

TOTAL SPENT:

MONTHLY SAVING:

MONTHLY INVESTMENT:

BILLS CHECKLIST

✓	BILL	AMOUNT	DUE DATE
☐			
☐			
☐			
☐			
☐			
☐			
☐			
☐			
☐			
☐			
☐			
☐			

DAILY EXPENSES

MONTH OF

DATE	DESCRIPTION	CATEGORY	AMOUNT
		TOTAL	

DAILY EXPENSES

MONTH OF

DATE	DESCRIPTION	CATEGORY	AMOUNT
		TOTAL	

DAILY EXPENSES

MONTH OF

DATE	DESCRIPTION	CATEGORY	AMOUNT
		TOTAL	

DAILY EXPENSES

MONTH OF

DATE	DESCRIPTION	CATEGORY	AMOUNT
			TOTAL

notes

notes

MONTHLY BUDGET

JAN FEB MAR APR MAY JUN JUL AUG SEP OCT NOV DEC

INCOME

BILLS/UTILITIES		

INSURANCE

SHOPPING
WK 1
WK 2
WK 3
WK 4

GROCERIES/EATING OUT		

DEBT

TRANSPORTATION
WK 1
WK 2
WK 3
WK 4

SAVINGS

OTHER EXPENSES			

DONATIONS

TOTAL INCOME:

TOTAL SPENT:

MONTHLY SAVING:

MONTHLY INVESTMENT:

BILLS CHECKLIST

✓	BILL	AMOUNT	DUE DATE
☐			
☐			
☐			
☐			
☐			
☐			
☐			
☐			
☐			
☐			
☐			
☐			

DAILY EXPENSES

MONTH OF

DATE	DESCRIPTION	CATEGORY	AMOUNT
			TOTAL

DAILY EXPENSES

MONTH OF

DATE	DESCRIPTION	CATEGORY	AMOUNT
		TOTAL	

DAILY EXPENSES

MONTH OF

DATE	DESCRIPTION	CATEGORY	AMOUNT
		TOTAL	

DAILY EXPENSES

MONTH OF

DATE	DESCRIPTION	CATEGORY	AMOUNT
			TOTAL

notes

notes

MONTHLY BUDGET

JAN FEB MAR APR MAY JUN JUL AUG SEP OCT NOV DEC

INCOME

BILLS/UTILITIES		

INSURANCE

SHOPPING	
WK 1	
WK 2	
WK 3	
WK 4	

GROCERIES/EATING OUT		

DEBT

TRANSPORTATION	
WK 1	
WK 2	
WK 3	
WK 4	

SAVINGS

OTHER EXPENSES			

DONATIONS

TOTAL INCOME:

TOTAL SPENT:

MONTHLY SAVING:

MONTHLY INVESTMENT:

BILLS CHECKLIST

✔	BILL	AMOUNT	DUE DATE

DAILY EXPENSES

MONTH OF

DATE	DESCRIPTION	CATEGORY	AMOUNT
			TOTAL

DAILY EXPENSES

MONTH OF

DATE	DESCRIPTION	CATEGORY	AMOUNT
			TOTAL

DAILY EXPENSES

MONTH OF

DATE	DESCRIPTION	CATEGORY	AMOUNT
			TOTAL

DAILY EXPENSES

MONTH OF

DATE	DESCRIPTION	CATEGORY	AMOUNT
			TOTAL

notes

notes

MONTHLY BUDGET

JAN FEB MAR APR MAY JUN JUL AUG SEP OCT NOV DEC

INCOME

BILLS/UTILITIES		

INSURANCE

SHOPPING
WK 1
WK 2
WK 3
WK 4

GROCERIES/EATING OUT		

DEBT

TRANSPORTATION
WK 1
WK 2
WK 3
WK 4

SAVINGS

OTHER EXPENSES			

DONATIONS

TOTAL INCOME:

TOTAL SPENT:

MONTHLY SAVING:

MONTHLY INVESTMENT:

BILLS CHECKLIST

✓	BILL	AMOUNT	DUE DATE

DAILY EXPENSES

MONTH OF

DATE	DESCRIPTION	CATEGORY	AMOUNT
			TOTAL

DAILY EXPENSES

MONTH OF

DATE	DESCRIPTION	CATEGORY	AMOUNT
			TOTAL

DAILY EXPENSES

MONTH OF

DATE	DESCRIPTION	CATEGORY	AMOUNT
			TOTAL

DAILY EXPENSES

MONTH OF

DATE	DESCRIPTION	CATEGORY	AMOUNT
			TOTAL

notes

notes

MONTHLY BUDGET

JAN FEB MAR APR MAY JUN JUL AUG SEP OCT NOV DEC

INCOME

BILLS/UTILITIES		

INSURANCE

SHOPPING
WK 1
WK 2
WK 3
WK 4

GROCERIES/EATING OUT		

DEBT

TRANSPORTATION
WK 1
WK 2
WK 3
WK 4

SAVINGS

OTHER EXPENSES			

DONATIONS

TOTAL INCOME:

TOTAL SPENT:

MONTHLY SAVING:

MONTHLY INVESTMENT:

BILLS CHECKLIST

✔	BILL	AMOUNT	DUE DATE
☐			
☐			
☐			
☐			
☐			
☐			
☐			
☐			
☐			
☐			
☐			
☐			

DAILY EXPENSES

MONTH OF

DATE	DESCRIPTION	CATEGORY	AMOUNT
			TOTAL

DAILY EXPENSES

MONTH OF

DATE	DESCRIPTION	CATEGORY	AMOUNT
			TOTAL

DAILY EXPENSES

MONTH OF

DATE	DESCRIPTION	CATEGORY	AMOUNT
			TOTAL

DAILY EXPENSES

MONTH OF

DATE	DESCRIPTION	CATEGORY	AMOUNT
			TOTAL

notes

notes

MONTHLY BUDGET

JAN FEB MAR APR MAY JUN JUL AUG SEP OCT NOV DEC

INCOME

BILLS/UTILITIES		

INSURANCE

SHOPPING
WK 1
WK 2
WK 3
WK 4

GROCERIES/EATING OUT		

DEBT

TRANSPORTATION
WK 1
WK 2
WK 3
WK 4

SAVINGS

OTHER EXPENSES			

DONATIONS

TOTAL INCOME:

MONTHLY SAVING:

TOTAL SPENT:

MONTHLY INVESTMENT:

BILLS CHECKLIST

✓	BILL	AMOUNT	DUE DATE
☐			
☐			
☐			
☐			
☐			
☐			
☐			
☐			
☐			
☐			
☐			
☐			

DAILY EXPENSES

MONTH OF

DATE	DESCRIPTION	CATEGORY	AMOUNT
			TOTAL

DAILY EXPENSES

MONTH OF

DATE	DESCRIPTION	CATEGORY	AMOUNT
			TOTAL

DAILY EXPENSES

MONTH OF

DATE	DESCRIPTION	CATEGORY	AMOUNT
			TOTAL

DAILY EXPENSES

MONTH OF

DATE	DESCRIPTION	CATEGORY	AMOUNT
			TOTAL

notes

notes

MONTHLY BUDGET

JAN FEB MAR APR MAY JUN JUL AUG SEP OCT NOV DEC

INCOME

BILLS/UTILITIES		

INSURANCE

SHOPPING

WK 1	
WK 2	
WK 3	
WK 4	

GROCERIES/EATING OUT		

DEBT

TRANSPORTATION

WK 1	
WK 2	
WK 3	
WK 4	

SAVINGS

OTHER EXPENSES			

DONATIONS

TOTAL INCOME:

TOTAL SPENT:

MONTHLY SAVING:

MONTHLY INVESTMENT:

BILLS CHECKLIST

✔	BILL	AMOUNT	DUE DATE

DAILY EXPENSES

MONTH OF

DATE	DESCRIPTION	CATEGORY	AMOUNT
			TOTAL

DAILY EXPENSES

MONTH OF

DATE	DESCRIPTION	CATEGORY	AMOUNT
		TOTAL	

DAILY EXPENSES

MONTH OF

DATE	DESCRIPTION	CATEGORY	AMOUNT
		TOTAL	

DAILY EXPENSES

MONTH OF

DATE	DESCRIPTION	CATEGORY	AMOUNT
		TOTAL	

notes

notes

MONTHLY BUDGET

JAN FEB MAR APR MAY JUN JUL AUG SEP OCT NOV DEC

INCOME

BILLS/UTILITIES		

INSURANCE

SHOPPING

WK 1
WK 2
WK 3
WK 4

GROCERIES/EATING OUT		

DEBT

TRANSPORTATION

WK 1
WK 2
WK 3
WK 4

SAVINGS

OTHER EXPENSES			

DONATIONS

TOTAL INCOME:

TOTAL SPENT:

MONTHLY SAVING:

MONTHLY INVESTMENT:

BILLS CHECKLIST

✓	BILL	AMOUNT	DUE DATE
☐			
☐			
☐			
☐			
☐			
☐			
☐			
☐			
☐			
☐			
☐			
☐			

DAILY EXPENSES

MONTH OF

DATE	DESCRIPTION	CATEGORY	AMOUNT
			TOTAL

DAILY EXPENSES

MONTH OF

DATE	DESCRIPTION	CATEGORY	AMOUNT
		TOTAL	

DAILY EXPENSES

MONTH OF

DATE	DESCRIPTION	CATEGORY	AMOUNT
			TOTAL

DAILY EXPENSES

MONTH OF

DATE	DESCRIPTION	CATEGORY	AMOUNT
		TOTAL	

notes

notes

MONTHLY BUDGET

JAN FEB MAR APR MAY JUN JUL AUG SEP OCT NOV DEC

INCOME

BILLS/UTILITIES		

INSURANCE

SHOPPING

WK 1	
WK 2	
WK 3	
WK 4	

GROCERIES/EATING OUT		

DEBT

TRANSPORTATION

WK 1	
WK 2	
WK 3	
WK 4	

SAVINGS

OTHER EXPENSES			

DONATIONS

TOTAL INCOME:

TOTAL SPENT:

MONTHLY SAVING:

MONTHLY INVESTMENT:

BILLS CHECKLIST

✔	BILL	AMOUNT	DUE DATE
☐			
☐			
☐			
☐			
☐			
☐			
☐			
☐			
☐			
☐			
☐			
☐			

DAILY EXPENSES

MONTH OF

DATE	DESCRIPTION	CATEGORY	AMOUNT
			TOTAL

DAILY EXPENSES

MONTH OF

DATE	DESCRIPTION	CATEGORY	AMOUNT
			TOTAL

DAILY EXPENSES

MONTH OF

DATE	DESCRIPTION	CATEGORY	AMOUNT
			TOTAL

DAILY EXPENSES

MONTH OF

DATE	DESCRIPTION	CATEGORY	AMOUNT
			TOTAL

notes

notes

MONTHLY BUDGET

JAN FEB MAR APR MAY JUN JUL AUG SEP OCT NOV DEC

INCOME

BILLS/UTILITIES

INSURANCE

SHOPPING
WK 1
WK 2
WK 3
WK 4

GROCERIES/EATING OUT

DEBT

TRANSPORTATION
WK 1
WK 2
WK 3
WK 4

SAVINGS

OTHER EXPENSES

DONATIONS

TOTAL INCOME:

TOTAL SPENT:

MONTHLY SAVING:

MONTHLY INVESTMENT:

BILLS CHECKLIST

✓	BILL	AMOUNT	DUE DATE

DAILY EXPENSES

MONTH OF

DATE	DESCRIPTION	CATEGORY	AMOUNT
			TOTAL

DAILY EXPENSES

MONTH OF

DATE	DESCRIPTION	CATEGORY	AMOUNT
			TOTAL

DAILY EXPENSES

MONTH OF

DATE	DESCRIPTION	CATEGORY	AMOUNT
			TOTAL

DAILY EXPENSES

MONTH OF

DATE	DESCRIPTION	CATEGORY	AMOUNT
			TOTAL

notes

notes

MONTHLY BUDGET

JAN FEB MAR APR MAY JUN JUL AUG SEP OCT NOV DEC

INCOME

BILLS/UTILITIES		

INSURANCE

SHOPPING

WK 1
WK 2
WK 3
WK 4

GROCERIES/EATING OUT		

DEBT

TRANSPORTATION

WK 1
WK 2
WK 3
WK 4

SAVINGS

DONATIONS

OTHER EXPENSES			

TOTAL INCOME:

TOTAL SPENT:

MONTHLY SAVING:

MONTHLY INVESTMENT:

BILLS CHECKLIST

✓	BILL	AMOUNT	DUE DATE
☐			
☐			
☐			
☐			
☐			
☐			
☐			
☐			
☐			
☐			
☐			
☐			

DAILY EXPENSES

MONTH OF

DATE	DESCRIPTION	CATEGORY	AMOUNT
		TOTAL	

DAILY EXPENSES

MONTH OF

DATE	DESCRIPTION	CATEGORY	AMOUNT
			TOTAL

DAILY EXPENSES

MONTH OF

DATE	DESCRIPTION	CATEGORY	AMOUNT
			TOTAL

DAILY EXPENSES

MONTH OF

DATE	DESCRIPTION	CATEGORY	AMOUNT
			TOTAL

notes

notes

MONTHLY BUDGET

JAN FEB MAR APR MAY JUN JUL AUG SEP OCT NOV DEC

INCOME

BILLS/UTILITIES		

INSURANCE

SHOPPING
WK 1
WK 2
WK 3
WK 4

GROCERIES/EATING OUT		

DEBT

TRANSPORTATION
WK 1
WK 2
WK 3
WK 4

SAVINGS

OTHER EXPENSES			

DONATIONS

TOTAL INCOME:

TOTAL SPENT:

MONTHLY SAVING:

MONTHLY INVESTMENT:

BILLS CHECKLIST

✓	BILL	AMOUNT	DUE DATE
☐			
☐			
☐			
☐			
☐			
☐			
☐			
☐			
☐			
☐			
☐			
☐			

DAILY EXPENSES

MONTH OF

DATE	DESCRIPTION	CATEGORY	AMOUNT
		TOTAL	

DAILY EXPENSES

MONTH OF

DATE	DESCRIPTION	CATEGORY	AMOUNT
		TOTAL	

DAILY EXPENSES

MONTH OF

DATE	DESCRIPTION	CATEGORY	AMOUNT
			TOTAL

DAILY EXPENSES

MONTH OF

DATE	DESCRIPTION	CATEGORY	AMOUNT
			TOTAL

notes

notes

www.ingramcontent.com/pod-product-compliance
Lightning Source LLC
Chambersburg PA
CBHW072028150726
47999CB00002B/795